the lover and her human

winnie nantongo

the lover and her human @ 2021 by Winnie Nantongo.
All rights reserved. Printed in the United States of America by Amazon. No parts of this book may be reproduced.

acknowledgments

i want to thank my friend Brian Macpherson and Tumwebaze Jonath for his work on the book cover design. without the assistance of these beautiful people involved, this book would not have been possible.

to you fellow lovers and humans

every human
is beautifully
scarred

contents

fall

break

heal

rise

fall

winnie nantongo

i can't hold you
beyond time
but my words will

the lover and her human

words,
spoken soft and sweet
from lips so soft
a strawberry treat

winnie nantongo

i'm not a poet
but i will feed
your lonesome heart
with joyful words

the lover and her human

luscious words like vanilla
on her lips she'd do anything
to sample more of that taste
the aroma so inviting
she would be intoxicated
just by the thought

winnie nantongo

you asked
what my favorite color was
then i looked in your eyes
and there it was

the lover and her human

i'm a sucker
for those
beautiful
emerald green eyes
just like you, they are rare

winnie nantongo

always thought
i would die
a lonely soul
till you came
and changed
my mind

the lover and her human

you looked at me
and for a moment
i forgot who i was

winnie nantongo

our eyes close
breathless anticipation
then we let them touch
breathless
i feel your very essence
entwined with mine
do you like how it feels
my lips on yours

the lover and her human

i never liked
the taste of cherry
until i kissed your lips

winnie nantongo

i never knew
what love was
until my name
escaped your lips

the lover and her human

the sound
of your love
calling my
name
is too loud
to ignore

winnie nantongo

my soul
aspires to be
fluent in your
love language

the lover and her human

i want
to be as happy
as the thought of you
makes me

winnie nantongo

some nights
my dreams
stay awake
with me
as i drive
myself crazy
thinking
about you

the lover and her human

there are too many voices
in my head
but the thoughts about you
are the loudest

winnie nantongo

can i be
your happy
thoughts
at 3am
when you
can't sleep
or that's
too much
to ask

the lover and her human

breathe love
into my lungs
and romance
my soul
for my mind
is chained
in fear of
dying alone

winnie nantongo

when tomorrow comes
i hope it brings you along

the lover and her human

i was used
to being by myself
until you came along

winnie nantongo

my chaos
found shelter
in your heart

the lover and her human

you know it's real
when just their touch
calms your storms

winnie nantongo

your voice
quiets the chaos
in my mind

the lover and her human

your smile
is my sun
shine i bloom

winnie nantongo

7 billion faces
and yours
is my favorite

the lover and her human

i fell in love
with the
perfect mess
that you're

winnie nantongo

i knew
it was you
when my
feelings
for you
defeated
my ego

the lover and her human

is it weird that
my favorite place
is you

winnie nantongo

i will die wild
and in love

the lover and her human

i love who i be
when i'm with you

i don't say *i'm fine*
when my mind
is miles away

winnie nantongo

allow me
to undress
your heart
and taste
your love

the lover and her human

i'm either wine drunk
or drunk on love

winnie nantongo

you are the only
adventure
i wish to have

the lover and her human

some love
feels like poetry
and ours
is the living proof

winnie nantongo

even in a world
of the living
and ghosts
it will always be
me and you

the lover and her human

as we slow dance
to the music of our hearts
our souls entwine
a waltz of love

winnie nantongo

the sound
of your heartbeat
will always be
my soul's favorite music

the lover and her human

you're one hell of a song
i can never escape
always in my head
even when i'm not myself

winnie nantongo

you know how i taste
and the taste of all
the tears i have ever cried

the lover and her human

i haven't met
many people
in my life

but i would still
choose you
over and over again

winnie nantongo

if loving you
makes me a sinner
then i might as well
be called satan

the lover and her human

the devil and i
aren't friends
so i keep her close
to protect you
from her

winnie nantongo

i can't promise you
a forever with me
but i can promise
you a lifetime

the lover and her human

swimming in oceans
used to scare me
but if i knew
how amazing it felt

maybe
i would have met you
a bit earlier

break

the lover and her human

you cannot change
what you see
its image burned
deep inside you
until memory fails
a blessed relief
before death comes

winnie nantongo

as you walk
away from me
do not stop
be gone
like a memory
i never had

the lover and her human

the constant happiness
of true love
the deepest touch
of real passion
the absolute fulfillment
of emotional contentment
i knew these
not anymore
now you're gone

winnie nantongo

you kissed me
goodbye
but you never left

been seeing you
every time
i close my eyes

the lover and her human

love is the
scariest road
when you're
driving solo

winnie nantongo

in loving you
i experienced
both heaven
and hell

the lover and her human

had i met you earlier
may be i wouldn't know
what it feels like
to feel nothing
and everything
all at once

winnie nantongo

in a very short time
you have made me
feel everything
the love and the hurt

the lover and her human

i got distracted
staring into your eyes
that i forgot to look
into your heart

winnie nantongo

you hurt me
then say you love me
like that will make
the pain fade away

- not your toy

the lover and her human

when i say i'm done
you say you're down
i try to move away
but you pull me back
and when i need you
i find you gone

winnie nantongo

you hunt me
only to hurt me

the lover and her human

what do i do
when loving you
does nothing
but hurt

winnie nantongo

falling for you
was easy
but loving you
is hard

the lover and her human

if our love
was right
it wouldn't hurt
but heal

winnie nantongo

but darling
you can't
edit your feelings

the lover and her human

thought
you loved me
for my wildness
but now
you want to tame
my fire

winnie nantongo

i crave a love
that won't try
to change me

- *love me for me*

the lover and her human

kept the doors
to my heart open
for you for so long
and now
my hands are tired

- i'm letting go

winnie nantongo

maybe
i deserved better
but i wanted you

the lover and her human

i lost me
trying to be
perfect for you

winnie nantongo

because of you
my self esteem
became too heavy
to carry

the lover and her human

you were a dream
which came to life
but a memory now

winnie nantongo

erasing you
in my life
still left a mark
on my heart

the lover and her human

your existence
makes me believe
that perhaps
this heart
still beats for a reason

winnie nantongo

even when my mind
gave up on you
my heart did not

the lover and her human

i was madly
in love with you
but you were poison
to my soul

- *toxic*

winnie nantongo

with you
all sunny days were grey
the sun that warms you
dries me

the lover and her human

on coffee breaks
is how i met you
seven months
napkins held our little secret
and now
i turn to watch your face
on my pillow
my fingers penning
my favorite words
inside of you
choreographing moves
i never learnt
searching for oceans
i couldn't get
earning a symphony
of chuckles instead
i could feel it coming

winnie nantongo

was i too much
not beautiful enough
pushed you too hard
loved you so much
or it was
everything about me

the lover and her human

maybe i was too young
or just stupid
not to taste your lies
off your tongue
even when we kissed

winnie nantongo

stumbling blindly
searching to impress
my fingers writing clumsily
inside the perfection of her
my need for validity
driving my amateur pennings
i find rock pools
not deep oceans

the lover and her human

she was
pools of honey
and oceans
of sunsets

winnie nantongo

that's my problem
always searching for you
in everyone i meet

looking for the beauty and magic
that i saw in you

the lover and her human

thanks to you
i found comfort
in sad love songs

winnie nantongo

our song
doesn't sound
the same anymore

the lover and her human

i allowed you
into my heart
just for you
to walk out
of my life

winnie nantongo

you broke me
but babe
you will always
have your place
in my arms

the lover and her human

my heart
is my worst enemy
always falling for lovers
who do nothing
but break me

winnie nantongo

you burn me to ashes
then question
where my fire is
ashes don't burn

the lover and her human

i'm always falling
for those out of reach

winnie nantongo

you are not
even mine
but just the thought
of you and her
ruins my soul

- jealousy

the lover and her human

even though
you are not mine
i'm already yours

winnie nantongo

you open your legs for him
because that's the only way
to have him close
and then you call that love

the lover and her human

my heart
aches in silence
for the love
i thought i had
but never did

winnie nantongo

why can't i move on
from someone
i never had

the lover and her human

my mind is tired
of chasing
a thought of you

winnie nantongo

i knew
everything
comes to an end
just didn't know
even you and me

the lover and her human

i don't hate you for
leaving but i hate myself
for hoping you'd come
back

winnie nantongo

some nights
i lay in the bed at night
staring up at the ceiling
unable to sleep
i'm not wondering why you left
that doesn't bother me anymore
but what bothers me is *why?*
why i'm i still holding
onto the thought of
seeing you again
even though you left
without saying goodbye
why am i not angry at you
even though i should be

- i have questions you will never answer

the lover and her human

even after
all these years
i still can't
let anyone in
the way i did
with you

- *damaged*

winnie nantongo

i held onto you
when we were
falling apart
pulled you closer
even though it did hurt
i can still do it all over again
because that's the only feeling
i have ever known

the lover and her human

despite everything
you had me
and i had you

we had us
and that was enough

winnie nantongo

the brightest mornings
sometimes mask sadness
in plain sight
like make up
over old scars

the lover and her human

i'm afraid
our generation is broken
but masking the pain
with sad smiles

winnie nantongo

wish we could go
back in time
and say *screw it*
instead of letting go

the lover and her human

we might have
said our goodbyes
but i'm still not over you

winnie nantongo

for once
i desperately
want my absence
to matter to you

the lover and her human

you left
but the pain stayed
tell me how to
make it stop

winnie nantongo

i only look back
into my past
because that's where
i left you

the lover and her human

sometimes
the memory of a hello
hurts more than that
of a goodbye

winnie nantongo

i hope
you finally
found
what you couldn't
find in me

the lover and her human

at least
at one point
i was the reason
for your smile

winnie nantongo

when you meet someone
i hope she loves you
better than i can

the lover and her human

maybe
our forever
and ever place
doesn't exist

winnie nantongo

maybe
later
we will find
each other again

the lover and her human

we started out as strangers
to friends then lovers
and now we are back
to being strangers again

winnie nantongo

it's crazy
how some memories
turn into nightmares

the lover and her human

but how could we
promise each other
forever
when everything
evolves with time

and so do feelings
which move in phases
like the moon

heal

the lover and her human

sometimes
healing
starts with
walking away

winnie nantongo

walking away
from a toxic
relationship
is part of
self-care
work too

the lover and her human

the heartbreak
aged my soul
but i guess
i deserved
a little pain
to know
what i'm worth

winnie nantongo

with these words
i'm reconnecting
all the pieces
you left broken in me

the lover and her human

the more
i write
the more
i process
the hurt

winnie nantongo

went through
a series of hurt
to finally
find me again

the lover and her human

letting you go
didn't mean i stopped
loving you
i was choosing myself

- *self-love first*

winnie nantongo

i left
but my mind
keeps wandering
back to you

the lover and her human

believe me
it's been so hard
wanting you back
but convincing myself
that i don't

winnie nantongo

sometimes
i talk about you
and smile like
it no longer hurts

the lover and her human

never again
will i run back
into the hands
that couldn't
catch me then

winnie nantongo

i will never

regret loving you
but will always regret staying
even when you made me feel
like i meant nothing to you

the lover and her human

in a cold rush of emptiness
like a weight being lifted
my chest and my vision light
i realized
nothing we had before
matter now

- *you're my past and i'm my present*

winnie nantongo

because if you love someone
it's hard to let them go
but somethings are not meant to be
and if they are
then they will find their way
back to you

the lover and her human

one day
i will be able to talk
about what we had
and i won't cry this time

winnie nantongo

my favorite person
is a memory now

the lover and her human

you eventually
make it through
you heal
grow and smile again

winnie nantongo

been homesick lately
not for you
but for myself
this time

the lover and her human

i don't need you
to die for me
but to live for yourself
to me that's what love is

winnie nantongo

i know i did you wrong
and i'm trying to make it right
just didn't know what love meant
and i'm still learning

the lover and her human

i hope one day
you meet someone
who looks at you
the same way
you look at the stars.

- with so much adoration

winnie nantongo

my heart has been to war
with love a couple times
and every time
it's been left in pieces
but it still picks itself up
and goes to another

- *now that is living*

the lover and her human

i think you are strong
you are strong for letting yourself
fall every time
even after being hurt
by your past lovers

- you're a true lover

winnie nantongo

till now she is still
hoping it will be
you and her
in the end

- *hopelessly in love*

the lover and her human

sometimes
your soul only craves
for a hug from you

- *self-love*

winnie nantongo

i don't crave
to be seen but felt
so i share my soul
not my face

- *poetry is my escape*

the lover and her human

i'm not afraid of love
but i'm not making
the same mistake twice

- once bitten twice shy

winnie nantongo

you broke me once
what will stop you now

the lover and her human

it doesn't matter
how long it takes
for you to get
there

you will heal

winnie nantongo

i saw you
last night
but i didn't
feel anything

- *finally free*

the lover and her human

you stayed
for a while
but i'm still glad
we met

winnie nantongo

in the end
we were only
each other's
sometimes

the lover and her human

once upon a time
you meant everything
to me

the end

rise

the lover and her human

just like the sun
she promised
to rise again

winnie nantongo

when the time is right
you will find it

- *love*

the lover and her human

you are
your own
self place

winnie nantongo

there is freedom
in finally
letting go

the lover and her human

if he comes back
remember
he didn't choose you then

winnie nantongo

wait for someone
who you won't have
to beg to stay

the lover and her human

the right love
will stay

winnie nantongo

the right one
won't make you
choose them
before yourself

the lover and her human

no love will ever
make you feel whole
like the love
you give to yourself

winnie nantongo

i hope you never
stop loving yourself
no matter how many times
they try to make you
feel like shit

the lover and her human

you deserve someone
whose love is strong enough
to pick you up even on days
you can't hold yourself

winnie nantongo

i hope you find someone
who mindlessly plays with your hair
rubs your back
does the little things
and makes you feel fully secure
with yourself and your relationship

the lover and her human

be brave enough
to express your genuine feelings
and opinions
without caring to please a soul
what's so hard about matching
what you feel on the inside
with how you behave on the outside

winnie nantongo

don't be so quick
to look for love
in other places
when you haven't
found it in yourself yet

the lover and her human

you should always
be your first love
because no one
deserves your love
more than you do

winnie nantongo

you don't need him
to feel whole again
you were whole before him
and you have always been

the lover and her human

stop draining your energy
mothering little men

winnie nantongo

i don't wish you
to be a certain way
because expectations
breeds disappointments

the lover and her human

never love someone
too much
to an extent of
ignoring the truth
about them

winnie nantongo

love me
but not too much
to forget about yourself

the lover and her human

you can never
be enough for someone
who doesn't deserve you

winnie nantongo

the more you love yourself
the less you will beg
for others to love you

the lover and her human

i would settle
for a no
than a maybe

winnie nantongo

if you don't
fight for me
don't cry for me
when my broken pieces
find a home
in someone else's arms

the lover and her human

i hope
you find a home in you
and not in someone else's heart

about the writer

winnie is a writer, poet and creator born in Kampala, Uganda.
her stated goal is to assist people develop their minds and hearts
through creative expression. when she is not writing poems
or creating other art, she is engaging in social activism.

about the book

the lover and her human is a collection of poetry by winnie nantongo about love, loss, grief and empowerment divided into four sections; fall, break, heal and rise.

Made in the USA
Middletown, DE
27 December 2024